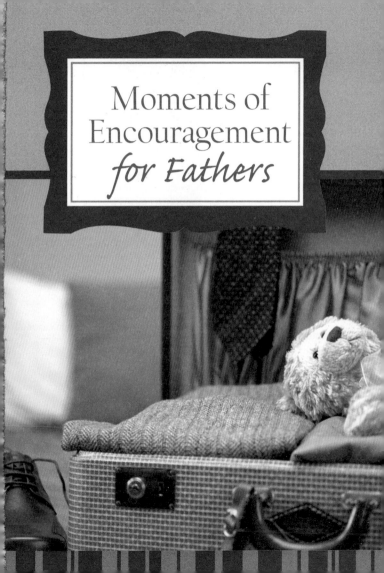

Moments of
Encouragement
for Fathers

© 2010 by Barbour Publishing, Inc.

Compiled by MariLee Parrish.

ISBN 978-1-60260-712-5

Scripture quotations marked NLT are taken from the *Holy Bible*, New Living Translation, copyright © 1996, 2004. Used by permission of Tyndale House Publishers, Inc. Wheaton, Illinois 60189, U.S.A. All rights reserved.

Scripture quotations marked NKJV are taken from the New King James Version®. Copyright © 1982 by Thomas Nelson, Inc. Used by permission. All rights reserved.

Scripture quotations marked KJV are taken from the King James Version of the Bible.

Scripture quotations marked NIV are taken from the HOLY BIBLE, NEW INTERNATIONAL VERSION®. NIV®. Copyright © 1973, 1978, 1984 by International Bible Society. Used by permission of Zondervan. All rights reserved.

Cover image: Stephanie Cabrera/Cusp/Corbis

Published by Barbour Publishing, Inc., P.O. Box 719, Uhrichsville, Ohio 44683, www.barbourbooks.com

Our mission is to publish and distribute inspirational products offering exceptional value and biblical encouragement to the masses.

ecpa Member of the
Evangelical Christian
Publishers Association

Printed in India.

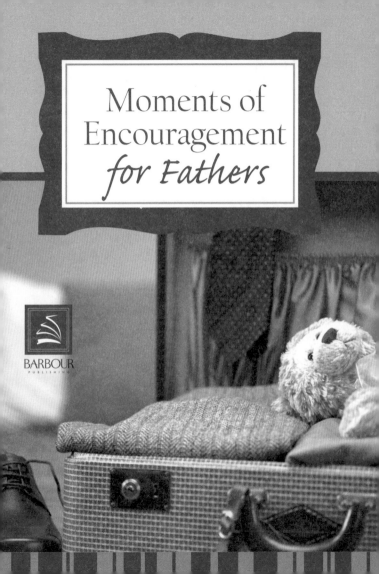

Moments of
Encouragement
for Fathers

BARBOUR
PUBLISHING

Don

Sending this to you for your birthday. I got a book for each son-in-law. I trust you will use it to be a thoughtful encouragment to you. Brad, Nolan & Mary are far to precious to all of us to spend their lives feeling they can not measure up. On day 224 one reads that being happy is so very important. We may have made this mistake - perhaps thats why we see things more clearly!

mom
2013

LOVINGLY

If parents behave lovingly toward their children,
combining mercy with loving discipline,
and loving discipline with fatherly and motherly
compassion, they are more likely to save their
children's hearts than if they were stern and
short-tempered. Our children must still make their
own eternal decisions for themselves—but at least
we will know, whatever they should choose, that
in love we have done all that we could to keep our
children safe.

—JOHN BUNYAN

POSITIVE KIDS

When you put faith, hope, and love together,
you can raise positive kids in a negative world.

—ZIG ZIGLAR

MY RESPONSIBILITY

It isn't important for me to know the destination
or even the path that I will be taking to get there;
He who I am following knows the way.
My responsibility is simply to follow.

—DARLENE SALA

WHAT IS A FATHER?

F. . .you are my friend.
A. . .you are my ally.
T. . .you are my teacher.
H. . .you are my hero.
E. . .you are my example.
R. . .you are my rock.

—K. WILLIAMS

More Important Things

Father, I often become too concerned with the mundane aspects of my children's lives—clothes, sports, money, and school. I pray that I go beyond my checklists of everyday matters to the more important spiritual subjects. I pray that my children are traveling with You as we journey along the road of life. Amen.

We Don't Have Long

Daddy, come and play with me;
I won't be small for long.
Come watch and see what I can do;
Soon I'll be big and strong.

—MARILEE PARRISH

CHILDREN OF GOD

Let us look upon our children, let us love them
and train them as children of the covenant and
children of the promise—these are the children
of God.

—ANDREW MURRAY

PLACE EVERYTHING IN GOD'S HANDS

I have held many things in my hands and have lost them all, but whatever I have placed in God's hands, that I still possess.

—MARTIN LUTHER

GOD, THE FATHER

A child identifies his parents with God, whether the adults want that role or not. Most children "see" God the way they perceive their earthly fathers.

—JAMES DOBSON

TIME AND SUPPORT

Father, when my children were learning to walk, I held them up to keep them from falling. As they get older, they'll still need my time and support to ensure their successes in life. Help me prepare my children for their future. Amen.

A WORTHY PURPOSE

Many persons have a wrong idea of what constitutes true happiness. It is not attained through self-gratification but through fidelity to a worthy purpose.

—HELEN KELLER

LISTEN

If we as parents are too busy to listen to our
children, how then can they understand a God
who hears?

—V. GILBERT BEERS

ROOTS AND WINGS

There are only two things we should give our children. One is roots; the other, wings.

—HODDING CARTER

AN IMAGE OF
THE FATHER

Can't you see the Creator of the universe,
who understands every secret, every mystery,
sitting patiently and listening to a four-year-old
talk to him? That's a beautiful image of a father.

—JAMES DOBSON

THE ACTION OF LOVE

Heavenly Father, I want to love You, my significant other, my children, and my neighbors. Help me go beyond the "emotion" of love to the "action" of love. Amen.

THE MASTER'S WORKSHOP

The Christian home is the Master's workshop, where the processes of character molding are silently, lovingly, faithfully, and successfully carried on.

—LORD HOUGHTON

I WILL

When a man says "I will," it may not mean much.
We very often say "I will" when we don't mean to
fulfill what we say. But when we come to the
"I will" of Christ, He means to fulfill it. Everything
He promised to do, He is able and willing to
accomplish. I cannot find any scripture where He
says "I will" do this or "I will" do that but that it
will be done.

—DWIGHT L. MOODY

AWAKENING

There is so much that is beautiful and good to wake up to. Our children drive us toward this awakening.

—POLLY BERRIEN BERENDS

IN DEBT TO CHILDREN

I wonder if we who have grown up will ever
know on this side of the grave how much we
owe to children, who seem—but only seem—
to owe us so much.

—FRANCIS C. KELLEY

REMEMBER

Watch yourselves closely so that you do not forget the things your eyes have seen or let them slip from your heart as long as you live. Teach them to your children and to their children after them.

—DEUTERONOMY 4:9 NIV

GOD GIVES HIMSELF

Let a man think and care ever so little about God,
he does not therefore exist without God. God is
here with him, upholding, warming, delighting,
teaching him—making life a good thing to him.
God gives him Himself, though the man knows
it not.

—GEORGE MACDONALD

THE DECISION TO
HAVE A CHILD

Making the decision to have a child is
momentous. It is to decide forever to have your
heart go walking around outside your body.

—ELIZABETH STONE

THE SPIRIT OF LOVE

You will find, as you look back upon your life,
that the moments when you have really
lived are the moments when you have done
things in the spirit of love.

—HENRY DRUMMOND

GOD'S CHILD

As God's child, today is your best day because you
are totally and completely dependent upon Him. . . .
God is your only rock, your only security, your only
certainty, and your only hope.

—ROY LESSIN

ALWAYS THERE

Heavenly Father, how great You are because You
stand by me despite my shortcomings. I know
Your presence upholds me in the face of strong
opposition. Help me emulate You in being there for
my family. Amen.

PRECIOUS IN HIS SIGHT

Want to enter God's kingdom?
Then become like little children.
Want to be great in God's eyes?
Then become like little children.
Want to let Jesus know you welcome
    and receive Him?
Then welcome little children.

—ROY ZUCK

THE PRESENT

Children think not of what is past, nor what is to come, but enjoy the present time, which few of us do.

—JEAN DE LA BRUYÈRE

REACH FOR THE SUN

It's not only children who grow. Parents do, too. As much as we watch to see what our children do with their lives, they are watching us to see what we do with ours. I can't tell my children to reach for the sun. All I can do is reach for it myself.

—JOYCE MAYNARD

TO TEACH A CHILD

The parents exist to teach the child, but also they
must learn what the child has to teach them;
and the child has a very great deal to teach.

—ARNOLD BENNETT

TRUST

Father, I want my children to approach me as one who will help. I want them to trust me. If their childhood is rife with fear, they may find it more difficult to approach You. If they are suspicious of my goodness, they may be unable to clearly see Your goodness. Father, I cannot perfectly emulate You, but I pray that my children see enough of You in me that they grow into an understanding of Your true, loving nature. Amen.

LIGHT SWITCHES

Affirming words from moms and dads are like light switches. Speak a word of affirmation at the right moment in a child's life, and it's like lighting up a whole roomful of possibilities.

—GARY SMALLEY

SPIRITUAL CHILD

A parent must respect the spiritual person of his
child and approach it with reverence.

—GEORGE MACDONALD

A Child's View

For a new take on God's kingdom, spend time with a child today.

—PAMELA MCQUADE

SOME ASSEMBLY
REQUIRED

The difficult thing about children is that they come with no instructions. You pretty well have to assemble them on your own.

—JAMES DOBSON

DAY 35

WHAT MY FAMILY DESERVES

Lord, I am well aware that I am often more considerate of my friends than I am of my own family. When I seek to please everyone else at the expense of my family, I know the emphasis is in the wrong place. I should rather gain the good opinion of my family than impress any friend. Help me to treat my family with respect, dignity, and consideration. Amen.

ATTITUDE IS
EVERYTHING

Your attitude about who you are and what you have is
a very little thing that makes a very big difference.

—THEODORE ROOSEVELT

THANK GOD FOR
YOUR CHILDREN

Have you taken time lately to thank God for
these wonderful gifts you call your children?
Or has life been so busy that you see them only as
challenges, as mischiefs, as time-eaters, as heavy
responsibilities, or as headaches and problems?

—TIM HANSEL

THE NOISE OF A CHILD

A child enters your home and for the next twenty years makes so much noise you can hardly stand it. The child departs, leaving the house so silent you think you are going mad.

—JOHN ANDREW HOLMES

TIME

When we love something, it is of value to us; and when something is of value to us, we spend time with it, time enjoying it, and time taking care of it. . . . So it is when we love children; we spend time admiring them and caring for them. We give them our time.

—M. SCOTT PECK

REMAIN IN CHRIST'S LOVE

"If you obey my commands, you will remain in my love, just as I have obeyed my Father's commands and remain in his love."

—JOHN 15:10 NIV

A Truth of God

Wherever in anything that God has made, in the glory of it, be it sky or flower or human face, we see the glory of God. There a true imagination is beholding a truth of God.

—GEORGE MACDONALD

WISDOM

To be patient in little things, to be tolerant in large affairs, to be happy in the midst of petty cares and monotonies, that is wisdom.

—JOSEPH FORT NEWTON

LOVE

Love is active and sincere, courageous, patient,
faithful, prudent, and manly.

—THOMAS À KEMPIS

IN CHECK

Children keep us in check. Their laughter prevents our hearts from hardening. Their dreams ensure we never lose our drive to make ours a better world. They are the greatest disciplinarians known to mankind.

—QUEEN RANIA OF JORDAN

CONSTANT SUPPORT

Father, I pray that neither my family nor I ever stand so sure of ourselves that we think we can never stumble. May we always be willing to seek Your comfort and support. Amen.

SUPPORT AND FREEDOM

The hardest part of raising a child is teaching them
to ride bicycles. A shaky child on a bicycle for the
first time needs both support and freedom.
The realization that this is what the child will
always need can hit hard.

—SLOAN WILSON

LEAD THE WAY

If you want your child to walk the righteous path,
do not merely point the way—lead the way.

—J. A. ROSENKRANZ

PARENT TEACHER

The Hebrew word for parents is *horim*, and it comes from the same root as *moreh*, "teacher." The parent is, and remains, the first and most important teacher that the child will have.

—RABBI KASSEL ABELSON

HUMAN NATURE

You don't really understand human nature unless
you know why a child on a merry-go-round will
wave at his parents every time around—and why
his parents will always wave back.

—WILLIAM D. TAMMEUS

FAMILY TIME

Father, help me reschedule my time to put the important things first. The time that I spend with You and my family should take precedence over urgent matters that become meaningless after the deadline has passed. Amen.

CHILD RAISING

The guys who fear becoming fathers don't understand that fathering is not something perfect men do, but something that perfects the man. The end product of child raising is not the child but the parent.

—FRANK PITTMAN

PERCEPTIVE CHILDREN

Children are very nice observers and will often perceive your slightest defect.

—FRANÇOIS DE FENELON

HAPPINESS

Happiness is to be found only in the home where God is loved and honored, where each one loves and helps and cares for the others.

—THÉOPHANE VÉNARD

HOW MUCH LOVE?

I am not sure exactly what heaven will be like, but I
don't know that when we die and it comes time for
God to judge us, He will *not* ask, "How many good
things have you done in your life?" Rather He will ask,
"How much *love* did you put into what you did?"

—MOTHER TERESA

GOD'S PROMISES

Father, thank You for giving all the world a visible sign of Your covenant that stretches across the heavens after a rain. All people can see and know that You keep Your promises. I pray that every time my children see a rainbow they will rejoice and be reassured that their Creator loves and cares for them. Amen.

MY FAMILY: A CHURCH

Every Christian family ought to be, as it were, a little church consecrated to Christ and wholly influenced and governed by His rules.

—JONATHAN EDWARDS

MIMICS

Children are natural mimics—they act like their parents in spite of every attempt to teach them good manners.

—BOB KELLY

INTEGRITY

Live so that when your children think of fairness
and integrity, they think of you.

—H. JACKSON BROWN JR.

WATCH YOUR WORDS

Even when you think your children aren't listening, they are. Choose your words carefully!

—MARILEE PARRISH

SALVATION

"For God so loved the world that he gave his one and only Son, that whoever believes in him shall not perish but have eternal life."

—JOHN 3:16 NIV

FINDING THE
RIGHT WAY

If you haven't time to help youngsters find the right way in life, somebody with more time will help them find the wrong way.

—FRANK CLARK

ALL FUTURE
GENERATIONS

The words a father speaks to his children in the privacy of the home are not overheard at the time, but as in whispering galleries, they will be heard at the end and by posterity.

—JEAN PAUL RICHTER

ONLY YOUNG ONCE

You have a lifetime to work, but children are only young once.

—POLISH PROVERB

WHERE LOVE STARTS

It is easy to love the people far away. It is not always easy to love those close to us. . . . Bring love into your home, for this is where our love for each other must start.

—MOTHER TERESA

HOPE

Father, I do not know what changes the future will bring, but I know You will take care of the things that concern me today and protect me from what may come against me tomorrow. You bring me hope. Amen.

FOOTSTEPS

Parents who expect their children to follow in
their footsteps should be careful about dragging
their feet.

—REV. GEORGE HALL

PART OF OURSELVES

When we choose to be parents, we accept
another human being as part of ourselves. . . .
From that time on, there will be another person
on this earth whose orbit around us will affect
us as surely as the moon affects the tides,
and affect us in some ways more deeply than
anyone else can.

—FRED ROGERS

SENSE OF WONDER

If a child is to keep alive his inborn sense of wonder, he needs the companionship of at least one adult who can share it, rediscovering with him the joy, excitement, and mystery of the world we live in.

—RACHEL CARSON

A RIGHT HEART

Great beauty, great strength, and great riches
are really and truly of no great use; a right heart
exceeds all.

—BENJAMIN FRANKLIN

SERENITY

Father, help me to develop the serenity that produces a calming influence on others, especially the members of my family. By trusting in Your guidance, we can overcome any crisis. Amen.

BE A GREAT TEACHER

One father is worth more than a hundred schoolmasters.

—GEORGE HERBERT

A SHORT MOMENT

Our children are here to stay, but our babies and toddlers and preschoolers are gone as fast as they can grow up—and we have only a short moment with each. When you see a grandfather take a baby in his arms, you see that the moment hasn't always been long enough.

—ST. CLAIR ADAMS SULLIVAN

MAKE A
DIFFERENCE NOW

If we are going to make a difference as fathers, we
need to do it now. The decision is practical.
It has to do with bedtimes, Saturday football
games, stories, and hamburgers; and it has to do
with carving those times out of busy lives—today.

—ROB PARSONS

THE FUTURE

We cannot always build the future for our youth,
but we can build our youth for the future.

—FRANKLIN D. ROOSEVELT

GOD'S WILL FOR
A FATHER

Lord, I am most happy when I clearly identify
what You want me to do and I go about doing
it with all my strength. Happiness as a father
is leading my family in Your ways and working
vigorously to earn their respect and love.
Amen.

BE A BLESSING

Pray that you may be an example and a blessing unto others and that you may live more to the glory of your Master.

—CHARLES H. SPURGEON

RESPONSIBILITY AND TRUST

Few things help an individual more than to place responsibility upon him and to let him know that you trust him.

—BOOKER T. WASHINGTON

FINDING THEIR WAY

Don't laugh at a youth for his affectations; he is only trying on one face after another to find his own.

—LLOYD LOGAN PEARSALL SMITH

THE YEARS GO BY FAST

Try not to miss a moment of your little person's life. The days might seem long, but remember: The years go by fast!

—MARILEE PARRISH

COMPASSION

As a father has compassion on his children, so the LORD has compassion on those who fear him.

—PSALM 103:13 NIV

STAND-IN MOMMY

There are very good reasons for Dad to be there. . . .
They tend to play a little more, they roughhouse,
they tease, they help you deal with your frustrations,
they don't always gratify your needs in the way you
want, and yet this can help you feel that you're going
to be okay when you're apart from your mommy.

—KYLE PRUETT, MD

"COME HOME, FATHER"

Father, dear father, come home with me now,
The clock in the belfry strikes one;
You said you were coming right home
  from the shop,
As soon as your day's work was done.

—HENRY CLAY WORK

VIRTUES

There is no doubt that it is around the family
and the home that all the greatest virtues,
the most dominating virtues of human society,
are created, strengthened, and maintained.

—SIR WINSTON CHURCHILL

MOLDED INTO LOVELINESS

Because God is so free from stain, so loving, so unselfish, so good, so altogether what He wants us to be, so holy, therefore all His works declare Him in beauty. His fingers can touch nothing but to mold it into loveliness.

—GEORGE MACDONALD

THE HEAVENLY COMPASS

Father, I pray that I will convey to my children a determination to follow the heavenly compass. May they be drawn to Your path and not depart from it. Amen.

A HIGH CALLING

Being a faithful child of God is our first calling.
Being faithful to our spouse and children is second.
Everything else comes after that.

—MARILEE PARRISH

GENERATIONS

One generation plants the trees; another gets the shade.

—CHINESE PROVERB

MORE TIME

In bringing up children, spend on them half as much money and twice as much time.

—UNKNOWN

A NURTURING FAMILY

Feelings of worth can flourish only in an
atmosphere where individual differences
are appreciated, mistakes are tolerated,
communication is open, and rules are flexible—
the kind of atmosphere that is found in a nuturing
family.

—VIRGINIA SATIR

THE CORRECT PATH

Father, You are at all of the intersections of my life.
You are there to show me the right way to go. I pray
that I'll recognize Your heavenly guidance and have
the commitment to follow the correct path. Amen.

THE SAME BLOOD

Children of the same family, the same blood
with the same first associations and habits,
have some means of enjoyment in their power,
which no subsequent connections can supply.

—JANE AUSTEN

A Unique Bond

When my father died and my two brothers and I sat down to talk about him, we discovered that we were talking about three different men—and I had never met the other two.

—UNKNOWN

A GOOD MANAGER

That energy which makes a child hard to manage is the energy which afterwards makes him a manager of life.

—HENRY WARD BEECHER

DELIGHTFUL SONGS

Glory to the Father give,
God in whom we move and live;
Children's prayers He deigns to hear;
Children's songs delight His ear.

—JAMES MONTGOMERY

A BEACON

Father, I pray that I serve as a beacon for my family. I pray that by recognizing me as a source of guidance, they will find the way to You as the shelter for their lives. Amen.

SMILE AT THE
ONES YOU LOVE

If you have only one smile in you, give it to the
people you love. Don't be surly at home then go out
in the street and start grinning "Good morning" at
total strangers.

—MAYA ANGELOU

ALWAYS WATCHING

Don't worry that children never listen to you;
worry that they are always watching you.

—ROBERT FULGHUM

REALIZATION

By the time a man realizes that maybe his father
was right, he usually has a son who thinks he's
wrong.

—CHARLES WADSWORTH

LOVE YOUR CHILDREN
AS THEY ARE

We can't form our children on our own
concepts; we must take them and love them as
God gives them to us.

—JOHANN WOLFGANG
VON GOETHE

JESUS LOVES THE
LITTLE CHILDREN

"Let the little children come to Me, and do not
forbid them; for of such is the kingdom of heaven."

—MATTHEW 19:14 NKJV

FORGIVENESS

Nothing brings families together faster than forgiveness. That should make it Step Number 1, but most of us find forgiving hard. We associate it with weakness and losing when, actually, the reverse is true. When you forgive, you gain strength and come out a winner.

—DR. JOYCE BROTHERS

A HERO

Every father is a hero in the eyes of his children.

—CONOVER SWOFFORD

HOME

Home is the one place in all this world where
hearts are sure of each other. It is the place of
confidence. . .where we pour out the unreserved
communications of full and confiding hearts.
It is the spot where expressions of tenderness
gush out without any sensation of awkwardness
and without any dread of ridicule.

—FREDERICK W. ROBERTSON

BE AN EXAMPLE

There is only one way to bring up a child in the
way he should go, and that is to travel that way
yourself.

—ABRAHAM LINCOLN

WISE AND DECISIVE

Dear Jesus, I want my choices to be in keeping with the examples set by You. But when the options appear equally valid, each having risks and benefits, I pray I will be both wise and decisive. Amen.

THE HAPPIEST MOMENTS
ARE AT HOME

The happiest moments of my life have been the few
which I have passed at home in the bosom of my
family.

—THOMAS JEFFERSON

GROUNDED

If you want children to keep their feet on the ground, put some responsibility on their shoulders.

—ABIGAIL VAN BUREN

EXTRAORDINARY

The most extraordinary thing in the world is an
ordinary man and an ordinary woman and their
ordinary children.

—G. K. CHESTERTON

FAMILY LIFE

Family life is full of major and minor crises. . . . It is tied to places and events and histories. With all of these felt details, life etches itself into memory and personality. It's difficult to imagine anything more nourishing to the soul.

—THOMAS MOORE

No More Reruns

Forgiving Lord, help me press on with my life. Reviewing reruns of my past serves no purpose. I shall not use past events as an excuse for my current shortcomings. With Your help, I will release the resentments I have carried so long and accept responsibility for my own actions. Amen.

PRAY TOGETHER

The simple exercise of praying together
regularly as a family will do more to strengthen
your family than anything else you could do
together.

—BRUCE BICKEL AND
STAN JANTZ

EVERYWHERE IS GOD

The earth underneath us is His hand upholding us. . . .
He tends us and cares for us; He is close to us, breathing
into our nostrils the breath of life, and breathing into our
spirit thoughts that make us look up and recognize the
love and care around us.

—GEORGE MACDONALD

GUARD YOUR SPARE TIME

Guard well your spare moments. They are like uncut diamonds. Discard them and their value will never be known. Improve them and they will become the brightest gems in a useful life.

—RALPH WALDO EMERSON

TIME AND LOVE

Time is. . .
Too slow for those who wait,
Too swift for those who fear,
Too long for those who grieve,
Too short for those who rejoice,
But for those who love,
Time is not.

—HENRY VAN DYKE

A FORGIVING GOD

Father, I sometimes make bad judgments and
sin against You. Within my own power,
I cannot correct them, but I trust in Jesus
to blot out all iniquities. When You remove
them, You don't leave a smudgy erasure or a
mismatched touch-up. Thank You for removing
my sins entirely so they no longer exist. Amen.

A Broken Nest

Any woodsman can tell you that in a broken and sundered nest, one can hardly find more than a precious few whole eggs. So it is with the family.

—THOMAS JEFFERSON

A Father's Time

A father's time means more to a child than all
the toys in the world. A father's time is a gift
unmatched by any other. It is never forgotten,
discarded, or unwanted.

—MARILEE PARRISH

YOU ARE THE EXAMPLE

The primary learning system for children is by
example, and you are often that example.

—CHRIS EWING

LIKE SNOW

Advice is like snow; the softer it falls,
the longer it dwells upon, and the deeper it
sinks into the mind.

—SAMUEL TAYLOR COLERIDGE

SERVING THE LORD

And if it seem evil unto you to serve the LORD,
choose you this day whom ye will serve;
whether the gods which your fathers served that
were on the other side of the flood, or the gods of
the Amorites, in whose land ye dwell: but as for me
and my house, we will serve the LORD.

—JOSHUA 24:15 KJV

GROWING OLD

If wrinkles must be written upon our brows,
let them not be written upon the heart.
The spirit should never grow old.

—JAMES A. GARFIELD

BEING SUCCESSFUL

I believe that being successful means having a balance of success stories across the many areas of your life. You can't truly be considered successful in your business life if your home life is in shambles.

—ZIG ZIGLAR

THE CHILD BECAME. . .

There was a child went forth every day,
and the first object he looked upon and
received with wonder or pity or dread, that
object he became,

And that object became part of him for the
day or a certain part of the day. . .or for many
years or stretching cycles of years. . . .

—WALT WHITMAN

TELL A STORY

Long before I wrote stories, I listened for stories. Listening for them is something more acute than listening to them. When their elders sit and begin, children are just waiting and hoping for one to come out, like a mouse from its hole.

—EUDORA WELTY

THE GRACE OF GOD

Sometimes the grace of God appears wonderfully
in young children.

—MATTHEW HENRY

YOUR CHILD IS
COURAGEOUS

Children are curious and are risk takers. They have lots of courage. They venture out into a world that is immense and dangerous. A child initially trusts life and the processes of life.

—JOHN BRADSHAW

INTO THE HEART

Children are a wonderful gift. . . . They have an extraordinary capacity to see into the heart of things and to expose sham and humbug for what they are.

—DESMOND TUTU

THE START OF A FAMILY

Where does the family start? It starts with a young man falling in love with a girl—no superior alternative has yet been found.

—SIR WINSTON CHURCHILL

RIGHT RESULTS

Work joyfully and peacefully, knowing that right thoughts and right efforts inevitably bring about right results.

—JAMES ALLEN

PUT ANGER IN ITS PLACE

Father, I pray that I learn not only to control my anger but also how to diffuse it and rid my mind of it. May I be an example to my family by putting anger in its place. Amen.

THE GREATEST OF ALL BLESSINGS

If you raise your children to feel that they can accomplish any goal or task they decide upon, you will have succeeded as a parent and you will have given your children the greatest of all blessings.

—BRIAN TRACY

YOUR CHILD'S
SELF-IMAGE

Once you see a child's self-image begin to improve,
you will see significant gains in achievement areas,
but even more important, you will see a child who
is beginning to enjoy life more.

—WAYNE DYER

TODAY

Many things can wait. Children cannot.
Today their bones are being formed, their blood is
being made, their senses are being developed.
To them we cannot say "tomorrow."
Their name is *today.*

—GABRIELA MISTRAL

YOUR CHILDREN'S MEMORIES

To be in your children's memories tomorrow,
you have to be in their lives today.

—BARBARA JOHNSON

FELLOWSHIP

Father, I know that it is impossible to know
what the future holds. I cannot direct my own
way. That is the reason I must depend on You.
I pray that I will center my objectives on being
in fellowship with You. Amen.

MANY GIFTS

I tell myself that God gave my children many gifts—spirit, beauty, intelligence, the capacity to make friends and to inspire respect. . . . There was only one gift He held back—length of life.

—ROSE KENNEDY

137

GOING AND DOING

Faith in Jesus Christ is to learn His ways by going
and doing them, not trying to understand them
first, or doing anything else whatever with them
first than obeying them.

—GEORGE MACDONALD

THE HONESTY
OF CHILDREN

Pretty much all the honest truth telling there is in
the world is done by children.

—OLIVER WENDELL HOLMES

A STEP IN THE UNKNOWN

It is familiarity with life that makes time speed quickly. When every day is a step in the unknown—as for children—the days are long with gathering of experience.

—GEORGE GISSING

SUCCESSFUL PLANS

All a man's ways seem innocent to him, but motives
are weighed by the LORD. Commit to the LORD
whatever you do, and your plans will succeed.
The LORD works out everything for his own ends.

—PROVERBS 16:2–4 NIV

LESSON FROM A CHILD

Many children are intuitively sensitive to people close to them. A child who is in her heart can know when a parent or buddy needs a kind word, a hug, or some friendly conversation.

—DOC CHILDRE

HELP THE FATHER'S CHILDREN

The service the Lord requires is not done in any church. He will not say to you, "You never went to church: Depart from me, I do not know you." But He will say, "Inasmuch as you never helped one of My Father's children, you have done nothing for Me."

—GEORGE MACDONALD

OPPORTUNITY

A pessimist sees the difficulty in every opportunity; an optimist sees the opportunity in every difficulty.

—SIR WINSTON CHURCHILL

A FULL HEART

We find delight in the beauty and happiness of
children that makes the heart too big for the body.

—RALPH WALDO EMERSON

LETTING GO

Heavenly Father, when it is time for my children to
seek their own way, I pray that the way they seek
and the path they find is in keeping with Your will.
Amen.

HOME

Where we love is home—home that our feet may leave, but not our hearts.

—OLIVER WENDELL HOLMES

GOD IS AWAKE

Have courage for the great sorrows of life and
patience for the small ones; and when you have
laboriously accomplished your daily task, go to
sleep in peace. God is awake.

—VICTOR HUGO

Thanksgiving

The arrogance of the young is a direct result of not having known enough consequences. The turkey that every day greedily approaches the farmer who tosses him grain is not wrong. It is just that no one ever told him about Thanksgiving.

—HARRY GOLDEN

LOVING THANKFULNESS

In our daily practice of prayer, we should begin
each day with an act of loving thankfulness to God.

—C. F. ANDREWS

DIVINE SUCCESS

Father, I wish to wisely use the time You have
entrusted to me. I must decide what the best use
of my time is. Help me recognize that time is too
precious to waste pursuing what the world defines
as success. Instead, direct me to invest my time
in developing closer harmony with my family and
with You. Amen.

SEARCHING FOR A
RELATIONSHIP

Children have taught me that no matter
what they say they are always searching for a
relationship with an adult that is challenging
and supportive for them. It's also crucial that
it's clear the relationship means something to
the grown-up, too.

—MICHAEL THOMPSON

LOVE AND LAUGHTER

Our homes should be filled with love and laughter,
a shining example of Christ's love in a dark world.

—MARILEE PARRISH

BIZARRE BEHAVIOR

No matter how calmly you try to referee, parenting
will eventually produce bizarre behavior, and I'm
not talking about the kids.

—BILL COSBY

A SPLENDID TORCH

Life to me is no brief candle; it is a sort of splendid torch which I have got hold of for the moment, and I want to make it burn as brightly as possible before handing it on to future generations.

—GEORGE BERNARD SHAW

COMMITMENT

Father, when I make a commitment, help me stand behind it. May I feel bound to bring the task to successful completion. Strengthen my resolve so I may be an example to my children. I want them to learn the importance of making a genuine effort to fulfill commitments. Amen.

GATHERING WEALTH

Could I climb to the highest place in Athens, I would lift my voice and proclaim, "Fellow citizens, why do you turn and scrape every stone to gather wealth and take so little care of your children to whom one day you must relinquish it all?"

—SOCRATES

CONNECTIONS

How many hopes and fears, how many ardent wishes and anxious apprehensions are twisted together in the threads that connect the parent with the child!

—SAMUEL G. GOODRICH

MANHOOD

A man's one claim on manhood is that he can call
upon God—not the God of any theology,
right or wrong, but the God out of whose heart
he came and in whose heart he is. This is his
highest power—that which constitutes his original
likeness to God.

—GEORGE MACDONALD

A CHILD'S HAND

What feeling is so nice as a child's hand in yours? So small, so soft and warm. . . A child's hand in yours—what tenderness and power it arouses. You are instantly the very touchstone of wisdom and strength.

—MARJORIE HOLMES

CHILDREN AND FATHERS

Children's children are the crown of old men;
and the glory of children are their fathers.

—PROVERBS 17:6 KJV

HEROES AND SONS

You don't raise heroes; you raise sons. And if you treat them like sons, they'll turn out to be heroes, even if it's just in your own eyes.

—WALTER SCHIRRA SR.

A HIGH ART

Listening is a high art of loving. Ask yourself,
*When was the last time I really listened to my
child?* . . . When someone is ready to share,
three magic words amplify your connection, and
they are: "Tell me more."

—REV. MARY MANIN MORRISSEY

LOOK FOR TRUTH

If you look for truth, you may find comfort in the
end; if you look for comfort, you will get neither
comfort nor truth, only soft soap and wishful
thinking to begin, and in the end, despair.

—C. S. LEWIS

MY REFUGE

You are my refuge.
Sometimes I run to You and hide.
You make all things new.
I put my trust in You.

—MARILEE PARRISH

A TENT OF BLESSINGS

Father, may my family and I develop shared Christian goals and spiritual values. May we have a long-term commitment to one another and to You. After my children become adults, may they still reside under the tent of Your blessings.

STRENGTH FROM GOD

God will give you the strength you need to
persevere. Don't be afraid to pick yourself back up
and try again.

—K. WILLIAMS

LOVE ALWAYS

Children need love, especially when they do not deserve it.

—HAROLD HULBERT

True Wealth

True wealth has little to do with money. A heart that is pure before God, a spouse who loves you, and children who admire you—that's true wealth.

—MARILEE PARRISH

MIRACLES

Miracles are a retelling in small letters of the very same story which is written across the whole world in letters too large for some of us to see.

—C. S. LEWIS

PATIENCE

Father, I trust in You. I pray that Your inner peace
will sustain me. My goal is neither the impatience
of rash actions nor the inaction of passive
resignation but the endurance of a mature Christian
who perseveres while awaiting Your will. Amen.

GREAT INFLUENCE

Small boys become big men through the
influence of big men who care about small boys.

—UNKNOWN

PLAN AHEAD

He who every morning plans the transaction of the day and follows out that plan carries a thread that will guide him through the maze of the most busy life. But where no plan is laid. . .chaos will soon reign.

—VICTOR HUGO

LOVE EACH OTHER

The most important thing a father can do for his children is to love their mother, and the most important thing a mother can do for her children is to love their father.

—UNKNOWN

WHAT A BABY
WILL DO. . .

A baby will make love stronger, days shorter,
nights longer, bankroll smaller, home happier,
clothes shabbier, the past forgotten, and the future
worth living for.

—UNKNOWN

GROWING IN CHRIST

Father, I want to daily renew myself spiritually.
I pray that I will manifest strength of character
to overcome those forces that get in my way of
growing in Your light. Amen.

PRAISE THEM

Love your children with all your hearts, love them enough to discipline them before it is too late. . . . Praise them for important things, even if you have to stretch them a bit. Praise them a lot. They live on it like bread and butter, and they need it more than bread and butter.

—LAVINA CHRISTENSEN FUGAL

LED BY GOD

Lord, I hide myself in You.
You are my rock, You are my refuge.
Lead me, guide me, walk beside me.

—MARILEE PARRISH

A MIRACLE OF LOVE

This is one of the miracles of love: It gives a power of seeing through its own enchantments and yet not being disenchanted.

—C. S. LEWIS

GROWING UP. . .

Sometimes we're so concerned about giving
our children what we never had growing up,
we neglect to give them what we did have
growing up.

—JAMES DOBSON

GOD'S CHILDREN

How great is the love the Father has lavished on us, that we should be called children of God! And that is what we are!

—1 JOHN 3:1 NIV

MAKE THE BEST OF IT

Take one thing with another, and the world is a pretty good sort of world, and it is our duty to make the best of it and be thankful.

—BENJAMIN FRANKLIN

EDUCATORS

Parents have become so convinced that educators
know what is best for their children that they
forget that they themselves are really the experts.

—MARIAN WRIGHT EDELMAN

THE GLORY OF PARENTHOOD

Parents are often so busy with the physical rearing of children that they miss the glory of parenthood, just as the grandeur of the trees is lost when raking leaves.

—MARCELENE COX

PEAT AND RE-PEAT

Children seldom misquote you. In fact, they usually repeat word for word what you shouldn't have said.

—UNKNOWN

LIFE AND GODLINESS

Father God, help me understand that You have
equipped me with everything I need to live as Your
child. May my family and I survive and thrive in
Your amazing love. Amen.

CHARITY

It is one of the most beautiful compensations
of this life that you cannot sincerely try to help
another without helping yourself.

—RALPH WALDO EMERSON

THE RIGHT ROAD

We all want progress, but if you're on the
wrong road, progress means doing an
about-turn and walking back to the right road;
in that case, the man who turns back soonest is
the most progressive.

—C. S. LEWIS

A Wise Word

Our children are not going to be just our
children—they are going to be other people's
husbands and wives and the parents of our
grandchildren.

—MARY S. CALDERONE

BAD COMPANY

Associate yourself with men of good quality if you esteem your own reputation; for it is better to be alone than in bad company.

—GEORGE WASHINGTON

THE POWER OF WORDS

Lord, I know that words are a powerful tool for strengthening people. The right words can build hope, restore confidence, and increase courage. Please give me the right words to inspire my children. Often, the only help I need to give them are words of encouragement. Amen.

I WILL. . .

I will supply the children with tools and knowledge to overcome the obstacles. I will pass on the wisdom of my years and temper it with patience. I shall impact in each child the desire to fulfill his or her dream.

—HENRY JAMES

A LIFE OF LOVE

Live your life so that when you die, others will
know that you loved others clearly,
loved your family dearly, and loved God
completely.

—BRUCE BICKEL AND STAN JANTZ

FIFTY YEARS FROM NOW

Fifty years from now it will not matter what kind of car you drove, what kind of house you lived in, how much you had in your bank account, or what your clothes looked like. But the world may be a little better place because you were important in the life of a child.

—UNKNOWN

GOD'S APOSTLES

A baby is born with the need to be loved—and never outgrows it. Children are God's apostles, day by day sent forth to preach of love and hope and peace.

—JAMES RUSSELL LOWELL

SERVING GOD

Heavenly Father, I pray that I will be single-minded so that when a situation calls for action, I will not hesitate to serve You. I pray that my children will recognize that decisions become easier once they develop the clear purpose to serve You first. Amen.

DAY
196

WORSHIP

Worship is living out our everyday lives to please
God. Let your kids see you worship every day, not
just on Sundays.

—MARILEE PARRISH

IMPACT

Those privileged to touch the lives of children and youth should constantly be aware that their impact on a single child may affect a multitude of others a thousand years from now.

—UNKNOWN

LET GOD HAVE CONTROL

Dear God, I pray that You would take control of my life today. Control my thoughts, my actions, and my time. Help me to be the best dad that I can be, and may I always point my family to You. Amen.

ASK GOD TO SHOW YOU THE WAY

Show me the way I should go.
For to You I lift up my soul.
Praise You, Jesus!
For Your unfailing love.

—MARILEE PARRISH

TRAINING THAT LASTS

Train up a child in the way he should go: and when he is old, he will not depart from it.

—PROVERBS 22:6 KJV

FILL A CHILD'S BUCKET

Parents need to fill a child's bucket of self-esteem so high that the rest of the world can't poke holes in it to drain it dry.

—ALVIN PRICE

RIGHT HABITS

In early childhood you may lay the foundation of poverty or riches, industry or idleness, good or evil by the habits to which you train your children. Teach them right habits then, and their future life is safe.

—LYDIA SIGOURNEY

THY WILL BE DONE

My God, give me neither poverty nor riches;
but whatsoever it may be Thy will to give,
give me with it a heart which knows humbly to
acquiesce what is Thy will.

—CHRISTIAN SCRIVER

BE A LIGHT

I love my father as the stars—he's a bright, shining example and a happy twinkling in my heart.

—ADABELLA RADICI

FATHER, REFRESH ME

Father, I ask not for easier tasks but for better ability to meet the assignments You give me. Refresh me daily with Your strength and love, and give me a loving nature that can help ease the burdens of others. Amen.

EXPLANATIONS

There's nothing that can help you understand your beliefs more than trying to explain them to an inquisitive child.

—FRANK A. CLARK

A FATHER'S EXAMPLE

I talk and talk and talk, and I haven't taught
people in fifty years what my father taught by
example in one week.

—MARIO CUOMO

FOOTPRINTS

Lives of great men all remind us,
We can make our lives sublime;
And, departing, leave behind us,
Footprints on the sands of time.

—HENRY WADSWORTH
LONGFELLOW

OPEN ARMS

My dear father! When I remember him, it is always
with his arms open wide to love and comfort me.

—ISOBEL FIELD

CHOICES AND CHALLENGES

Father, throughout life, I encounter situations that challenge me. As I examine each choice I must make, I pray that my desire will be to do what is right and that You will give me the strength to stand by my choice. Amen.

A NOURISHING HOME

Good, honest, hardheaded character is a
function of the home. If the proper seed is
sown there and properly nourished for a few
years, it will not be easy for that plant to be
uprooted.

—GEORGE A. DORSEY

IN THINE HANDS

My God! My time is in Thine hands. Should it please Thee to lengthen my life and complete, as Thou hast begun, the work of blanching my locks, grant me grace to wear them as a crown of unsullied honor.

—CHRISTIAN SCRIVER

REVERENCE AND RESPECT

He that will have his son have a respect for him and his orders must himself have a great reverence for his son.

—JOHN LOCKE

FRIENDSHIP AND LOVE

There is no friendship, no love like that of the parent for the child.

—HENRY WARD BEECHER

PROPER TRAINING

Father, it is difficult to overcome early training
that is bad, and it is difficult to go against
early training that is good. Help me give
proper training that will last a lifetime.
Allow me to show my children the proof of my
love for them through discipline that sets their
lives on the proper course. Amen.

THREE THINGS

The whole of Christianity is comprised in three things—to believe, to love, and to obey Jesus. These are things, however, which we must be learning all our life.

—CHRISTIAN SCRIVER

NO OTHER

Each of us is meant to have a character all our own, to be what no other can exactly be, and do what no other can exactly do.

—WILLIAM ELLERY CHANNING

MAKING A POINT

If you have an important point to make, don't try to be subtle or clever. Use a pile driver. Hit the point once. Then come back and hit it again. Then hit it a third time—a tremendous whack.

—WINSTON CHURCHILL

PRONE TO WANDER

Prone to wander, Lord, I feel it,
Prone to leave the God I love.
O to grace how great a debtor
Daily I'm constrained to be!
Let Thy goodness, like a fetter,
Bind my wandering heart to Thee.

—ROBERT ROBINSON

READING SCRIPTURE

By reading the scriptures, I am so renewed, that all nature seems renewed around me and with me. . . . The whole world is charged with the glory of God, and I feel fire and music under my feet.

—THOMAS MERTON

PROTECTOR

"Being a father" is something mythical and infinitely important: a protector, who would keep a lid on all the chaotic and catastrophic possibilities of life.

—TOM WOLFE

THE RICH AND POOR

Sometimes the poorest man leaves his children the richest inheritance.

—RUTH E. RENKEL

VOICES OF
THE DISTANT

God be thanked for books; they are the voices of the distant and the dead, and make us heirs of the spiritual life of past ages.

—WILLIAM ELLERY CHANNING

HAPPY DOING NOTHING

You are worried about seeing him spend his early
    years in doing nothing.
What! Is it nothing to be happy?
Nothing to skip, play, and run around all day long?
Never in his life will he be so busy again.

—JEAN-JACQUES ROUSSEAU

TALENTS AND SERVICE

Father, I pray that I can help my children recognize
their particular talents and give them the guidance
to enhance those talents. I pray that they will
happily accept the responsibility to serve others in
the way You have equipped them. May they learn
from me the joy of Christian service. Amen.

SONS-IN-LAW

One of life's greatest mysteries is how the boy who wasn't good enough to marry your daughter can be the father of the smartest grandchild in the world.

—JEWISH PROVERB

FUNDS OF LOVE

Let us more and more insist on raising funds of love, of kindness, of understanding, of peace. Money will come if we seek first the kingdom of God—the rest will be given.

—MOTHER TERESA

LOVE'S REWARD

Love seeks one thing only: the good of the one loved.
It leaves all the other secondary effects to take care
of themselves. Love, therefore, is its own reward.

—THOMAS MERTON

WISE CHILDREN

Your children tell you casually years later what it would have killed you with worry to know at the time.

—MIGNON MCLAUGHLIN

WORDS AND ACTIONS

Lord, I know that I have a duty to spread the
Gospel. Although actions speak louder than words,
actions without words are not enough. Help me
become dedicated to the Gospel, compelled to tell
others about the salvation found only in Jesus.
Let me start at home, so that my children realize
heir lives are not complete until they have become
Your children. Amen.

BRINGING UP CHILDREN

Before I got married, I had six theories about bringing up children; now I have six children and no theories.

—JOHN WILMOT

STANDING ON SHOULDERS

Each generation goes further than the generation preceding it because it stands on the shoulders of that generation. You will have opportunities beyond anything we've ever known.

—RONALD REAGAN

BY WHAT IS YOUR
LIFE SHAPED?

A life is either all spiritual or not spiritual at all.
No man can serve two masters. Your life is shaped
by the end you live for. You are made in the image
of what you desire.

—THOMAS MERTON

THE BEST PORTION

The best portion of a good man's life is his little,
nameless, unremembered acts of kindness and
love.

—WILLIAM WORDSWORTH

WHOLLY COMMITTED

Lord, give me a heart to be wholly committed to You as my Master. I actively dedicate myself to Your service. Build in me the strength for dedication that lasts beyond a few days or weeks and becomes a lifelong loyalty to my family and You. Amen.

JOINED FOR LIFE

What greater thing is there for human souls than
to feel that they are joined for life—to be with each
other in silent unspeakable memories.

—GEORGE ELIOT

FOOLS

Wisdom is the right use of knowledge. . . .
Many men know a great deal and are all the greater
fools for it. There is no fool so great a fool as a
knowing fool. But to know how to use knowledge
is to have wisdom.

—CHARLES SPURGEON

STRENGTH

Strength is not used rightly when it serves only to carry a man above his fellows for his own solitary glory. He is the greatest whose strength carries up the most hearts by the attraction of his own.

—HENRY WARD BEECHER

CHEERFUL BEAMS

O Holy Spirit, descend plentifully into my heart. Enlighten the dark corners of this neglected dwelling and scatter there Thy cheerful beams.

—SAINT AUGUSTINE

THE SUCCESS OF LOVE

The success of love is in the loving. . . . It is natural
in love to want the best for the other person,
but whether it turns out that way or not does not
determine the value of what we have done.

—MOTHER TERESA

PECULIAR AMBITION

Every man is said to have his peculiar ambition.
Whether it be true or not, I can say for one that
I have no other so great as that of being truly
esteemed of my fellow men, by rendering myself
worthy of their esteem.

—ABRAHAM LINCOLN

GRANDEUR OF CHARACTER

Grandeur of character lies wholly in force of soul, that is, in the force of thought, moral principle, and love, and this may be found in the humblest condition of life.

—WILLIAM ELLERY CHANNING

FATHERS AND SONS

It is not flesh and blood but the heart that makes us fathers and sons.

—JOHANN CHRISTOPH
FRIEDRICH VON SCHILLER

FRESH FROM GOD

I love these little ones, and it is not a slight thing
when they, who are so fresh from God, love us.

—CHARLES DICKENS

ETERNAL VALUES

Father, guide me as my children learn how to
distinguish between what is trivial and what is
vital. Help me teach them to focus their lives on
actions that will have eternal value. Amen.

THE ULTIMATE MEASURE

The ultimate measure of a man is not where he stands in moments of comfort and convenience, but where he stands in times of challenge and controversy.

—MARTIN LUTHER KING JR.

SOCIAL SERVICE

Perhaps the greatest social service that can
be rendered by anybody to the country and to
mankind is to bring up a family.

—GEORGE BERNARD SHAW

MEMORY'S LAMP

How confusing the beams from memory's lamp are;
One day a bachelor, the next a grampa.
What is the secret of the trick?
How did I get so old so quick?

—OGDEN NASH

BUILD WITH BOTH HANDS

He that gives good advice builds with one hand; he that gives good counsel and example builds with both.

—FRANCIS BACON

SELF-RESPECT

Father, the Bible is filled with examples of our
worth. You created us, You sacrificed Your Son for
us, and You were too kind to leave us without the
comfort of the Holy Spirit. In every aspect,
You have shown our value. Guide me as I work to
build self-respect in my children. Amen.

MAKING OTHERS GREAT

Great minds are to make others great.
Their superiority is to be used, not to break
the multitude to intellectual vassalage, not to
establish over them a spiritual tyranny, but to
rouse them from lethargy and to aid them to
judge for themselves.

—WILLIAM ELLERY CHANNING

AGE IS OPPORTUNITY

Age is opportunity no less,
Than youth itself, though in another dress;
And as the evening twilight fades away,
The sky is filled with stars, invisible by day.

—HENRY WADSWORTH
LONGFELLOW

PEACE OF MIND

There are many things that are essential to arriving at true peace of mind, and one of the most important is faith, which cannot be acquired without prayer.

—JOHN WOODEN

Prayer

I pray on the principle that wine knocks the cork out of a bottle. There is an inward fermentation, and there must be a vent.

—HENRY WARD BEECHER

Be Approachable

Father, sometimes my children have problems,
but because of their lack of experience,
they cannot express what is troubling them.
Their distress can go unnoticed unless I devote
time to being with them and talking with them.
Guide me in giving them the support they
need. Help them realize that they can make
their requests known to me—and to You.
Amen.

FATHER MEANS LOVE

To her, the name of Father was another name for love.

—FANNY FERN

Turning Point

We have come to a turning point in the road.
If we turn to the right, mayhap our children and
our children's children will go that way; but if we
turn to the left, generations yet unborn will curse
our names for having been unfaithful to God and to
His Word.

MONEY IS NOT ENOUGH

Let us not be satisfied with just giving money.
Money is not enough, money can be got, but they
need your hearts to love them. So, spread your love
everywhere you go.

—MOTHER TERESA

TODAY

No matter what looms ahead, if you can eat today, enjoy today, mix good cheer with friends today, enjoy it and bless God for it.

—HENRY WARD BEECHER

GOD'S INSTRUCTIONS

Fathers, do not exasperate your children;
instead, bring them up in the training and
instruction of the Lord.

—EPHESIANS 6:4 NIV

GOOD ADVICE

Don't be discouraged if your children reject your advice. Years later, they will offer it to their own offspring.

—UNKNOWN

HARD WORK

The heights by great men reached and kept
Were not attained by sudden flight;
But they, while their companions slept,
Were toiling upward in the night.

—HENRY WADSWORTH
LONGFELLOW

GREAT IS THY FAITHFULNESS!

Great is Thy faithfulness!
Morning by morning, new mercies I see.
All I have needed, Thy hand hath provided;
Great is Thy faithfulness, Lord, unto me!

—THOMAS O. CHISOLM

LOVE AND RESPECT

The love and respect of a child means more than
anything the corporate world could offer.

—MARILEE PARRISH

Expressions of Love

Heavenly Father, I thank You for Your continual, watchful eye upon me. Guide me to bring a concrete expression of love to others who have a physical or emotional crisis. Provide me with the wisdom to relieve the suffering of others. Amen.

A LIFETIME OF
MEMORIES

The memories we give may a lifetime live in the
hearts of those we hold so close.

—UNKNOWN

RECOUNTING GOD'S FAITHFULNESS

The key to receiving and living a life of hope, joy, and peace is recounting God's faithfulness out loud, quietly in your heart, and to others. When you begin to feel discouraged, exhausted, and at the end of your rope, *stop*; go before the throne of grace, and recall God's faithfulness.

—TINA C. ELACQUA

PARADOX

A king, realizing his incompetence, can either
delegate or abdicate his duties. A father can do
neither. If only sons could see the paradox, they
would understand the dilemma.

—MARLENE DIETRICH

A BETTER MAN

Any man worth his salt will stick up for what he
believes right, but it takes a slightly better man to
acknowledge instantly and without reservation
that he is in error.

—ANDREW JACKSON

SECURITY IN CHRIST

Father, a feeling of security is important at any age. I recognize Your strength as my protection. With the comfort of Your Word, I can put my daily concerns behind me. Thank You, Lord, for giving me the assurance of Your love and protection. Amen.

LONGING FOR HOME

As much as I converse with sages and heroes,
they have very little of my love and admiration.
I long for rural and domestic scene, for the
warbling of birds and the prattling of my
children.

—JOHN ADAMS

TWENTY YEARS
FROM NOW

Twenty years from now you will be more
disappointed by the things that you didn't do than
by the ones you did do. So throw off the bowlines.
Sail away from the safe harbor. Catch the trade
winds in your sails. Explore. Dream. Discover.

—MARK TWAIN

High Vocation

Sweetest Lord, make me appreciative of the dignity
of my high vocation and its many responsibilities.
Never permit me to disgrace it by giving way to
coldness, unkindness, or impatience.

—MOTHER TERESA

AFFLICTION

I would go to the deeps a hundred times to cheer a downcast spirit. It is good for me to have been afflicted, that I might know how to speak a word in season to one that is weary.

—CHARLES SPURGEON

A HEART OF MERCY

Father, I desire to be a more compassionate person. Help me to be kind and forgiving. Give me a heart full of mercy. Help me identify those ways in which I can serve others. Guide me to enlist the assistance of my family so they learn how to serve You by helping others. Amen.

SIXTY MINUTES

The future is something which everyone reaches at
the rate of sixty minutes an hour, whatever he does,
whoever he is.

—C. S. LEWIS

GROWING UP

When I was a boy of fourteen, my father was so ignorant I could hardly stand to have the old man around. But when I got to be twenty-one, I was astonished at how much the old man had learned in seven years.

—MARK TWAIN

DELIGHT

To show a child what once delighted you, to find the child's delight added to your own—this is happiness.

—J. B. PRIESTLEY

DISCIPLINE

Discipline doesn't break a child's spirit half as often as the lack of it breaks a parent's heart.

—UNKNOWN

GODLY REWARD

Sons are a heritage from the LORD, children a reward from him.

—PSALM 127:3 NIV

CHILDREN ARE MIMICS

Children are natural mimics who act like their
parents, despite every effort to teach them good
manners.

—UNKNOWN

A FATHER'S GREATNESS

It's only when you grow up and step back from [your father], or leave him for your own career and your own home—it's only then that you can measure his greatness and fully appreciate it. Pride reinforces love.

—MARGARET TRUMAN

BY YOUR OWN CONSENT

No power in society, no hardship in your condition can depress you, keep you down, in knowledge, power, virtue, influence, but by your own consent.

—WILLIAM ELLERY CHANNING

BEGINNINGS

So never lose an opportunity of urging a practical beginning, however small, for it is wonderful how often in such matters the mustard seed germinates and roots itself.

—FLORENCE NIGHTINGALE

INVESTMENTS

Father, as my children grow and develop,
their needs rapidly change. Provide me with
the skills and resources I need to promote their
continued growth. I invest my trust in You to meet
the physical, emotional, and spiritual needs of my
family. Help me make my first and most important
investment in my family. Amen.

Country Byways

My dear father, my dear friend, the best and wisest man I ever knew, who taught me many lessons and showed me many things as we went together along the country byways...

—SARAH ORNE JEWETT

HILLTOPS AND VALLEYS

The marvelous richness of human experience would lose something of rewarding joy if there were no limitations to overcome. The hilltop hour would not be half so wonderful if there were no dark valleys to traverse.

—HELEN KELLER

A SINGLE ACT

Others are affected by what I am and say and do,
so that a single act of mine may spread and spread
in widening circles, through a nation or humanity.

—WILLIAM ELLERY CHANNING

WINDS AND PRESSURE

When we long for life without difficulties,
remind us that oaks grow strong in contrary winds
and diamonds are made under pressure.

—PETER MARSHALL

REAL HEROES

Father, help me steer my children toward real
heroes—those who pursue righteousness.
Encourage my children to be heroic in upholding
the values that reflect Your will. Amen.

WATCH!

Watch your thoughts; they become your words.
Watch your words; they become your actions.
Watch your actions; they become your habits.
Watch your habits; they become your character.
Watch your character; it becomes your destiny.

—UNKNOWN

INSPIRATIONAL EXAMPLES

Nothing is so contagious as example, and our every really good or bad action inspires a similar one.

—FRANÇOIS DUC DE LA
ROCHEFOUCAULD

HUMAN MORALITY

A man does what he must—in spite of personal consequences, in spite of obstacles and dangers and pressures—and that is the basis of all human morality.

—WINSTON CHURCHILL

LOVE AND AUTHORITY

Between a man and his wife nothing ought to rule but love. Authority is for children and servants, yet not without sweetness.

—WILLIAM PENN

FAITHFULNESS

Father, may I be faithful in putting my trust in You. May my prayers for strength to overcome difficulties always come from an honest heart. Protect me from wavering as I follow You. Amen.

A FATHER'S HEART

There's no better feeling than knowing you are in
your father's heart and that you always will be.

—CONOVER SWOFFORD

QUESTIONS AND ANSWERS

You know children are growing up when they start asking questions that have answers.

—JOHN J. PLOMP

A Child's Injustice

There are two great injustices that can befall a child. One is to punish him for something he didn't do. The other is to let him get away with doing something he knows is wrong.

—ROBERT GARDNER

WHAT DOES LOVE LOOK LIKE?

It has the hands to help others. It has the feet to hasten to the poor and needy. It has eyes to see misery and want. It has the ears to hear the sighs and sorrows of men. That is what love looks like.

—SAINT AUGUSTINE

I SURRENDER ALL

All to Jesus I surrender,
All to Him I freely give:
I will ever love and trust Him,
In His presence daily live.
I surrender all.

—JUDSON W. VAN DEVENTER

DO YOUR PART

Educate your children to self-control, to the habit of holding passion and prejudice and evil tendencies subject to an upright and reasoning will, and you have done much to abolish misery from their future and crimes from society.

—BENJAMIN FRANKLIN

WONDERS

There are not seven wonders of the world in the eyes
of a child. There are seven million.

—WALT STREIGHTIFF

MISTAKES

The beauty of "spacing" children many years apart lies in the fact that parents have time to learn the mistakes that were made with the older ones—which permits them to make exactly the opposite mistakes with the younger ones.

—SYDNEY J. HARRIS

TOMBSTONES

A good character is the best tombstone. Those who loved you and were helped by you will remember you when forget-me-nots have withered.
Carve your name on hearts, not on marble.

—CHARLES SPURGEON

CONFIDENCE

Dear Lord, my confidence is built when I welcome You into my heart and mind and lay myself bare before You. Father, my trust is not in myself, but in You. Help me to lead my family with confidence. Amen.

THE BEGINNING OF LOVE

The beginning of love is to let those we love be perfectly themselves, and not to twist them to fit our own image. Otherwise we love only the reflection of ourselves we find in them.

—THOMAS MERTON

NEVER WASTED

Nothing you do for children is ever wasted.
They seem not to notice us, hovering,
averting our eyes; and they seldom offer thanks,
but what we do for them is never wasted.

—GARRISON KEILLOR

Riches

Many of us have inherited great riches from our parents—the bank account of personal faith and family prayers.

—NELS F. S. FERRE

WHERE LOVE IS. . .

For many people, the heavy responsibilities of
home and family and earning a living absorb all
their time and strength. Yet such a home—where
love is—may be a light shining in a dark place,
a silent witness to the reality and the love of God.

—OLIVE WYON

WORTHY GOALS

Help me to focus on the spiritual goals that will
honor You. Father, teach me how to use my time
and resources wisely so I will be a good example
for my children. Help me guide them so they will
make excellent choices for their lives and strive for
worthy goals. Amen.

CHARACTER INFECTION

Character is largely caught, and the father
and the home should be the great sources of
character infection.

—FRANK H. CHELEY

THE DAYS OF CHILDHOOD

Let me play in the sunshine;
Let me sing for joy;
Let me grow in the light;
Let me splash in the rain;
And remember the days of
My childhood forever.

—UNKNOWN

PERILS

When you face the perils of weariness, carelessness,
and confusion, don't pray for an easier life.
Pray instead to be a stronger man or woman of God.

—LUIS PALAU

A HEART AT REST

When the voices of children
Are heard on the green
And laughing is heard on the hill,
My heart is at rest within my breast
And everything else is still.

—WILLIAM BLAKE

CONTENTMENT

Lord, help me set worthy goals and encourage my children to do the same. But also guide us to set goals based on what You want us to do rather than what we imagine will bring pleasure, success, and contentment. Instead of looking forward in discontent, let us focus on what You have given us. May we see our cup as running over with Your blessings. Amen.

LASTING LEGACY

We are to love God wholeheartedly and teach our children to do the same. That's the kind of legacy that will last for generations and please God into eternity.

—BRUCE BICKEL AND STAN JANTZ

LOOKING BACK

We should not look back unless it is to derive
useful lessons from past errors, and for the purpose
of profiting by dearly bought experience.

—GEORGE WASHINGTON

BOUND BY LOVE

It is my pleasure that my children are free and happy, and unrestrained by parental tyranny. Love is the chain whereby to bind a child to his parents.

—ABRAHAM LINCOLN

TRUE GODLINESS

True godliness does not turn men out of the world, but enables them to live better in it and excites their endeavors to mend it.

—WILLIAM PENN

OUR GLORIOUS LORD

We will not hide these truths from our
children; we will tell the next generation about the
glorious deeds of the LORD, about his power and
his mighty wonders.

—PSALM 78:4 NLT

BELIEVE

Many children have gone further than they thought they could because a parent knew they could.

—UNKNOWN

ABOUT LOVE. . .

You ask me why God loves. You might as well ask me why the sun shines. It can't help shining, and neither can He help loving, because He is love Himself; and anyone that says He is not love does not know anything about love.

—DWIGHT L. MOODY

ONLY CHANCE

I expect to pass through this world but once;
any good thing therefore that I can do, or any
kindness that I can show to any fellow creature,
let me do it now; let me not defer or neglect it,
for I shall not pass this way again.

—STEPHEN GRELLET

ACCEPT THE BEST

Man finds it hard to get what he wants, because he does not want the best; God finds it hard to give, because He would give the best, and man will not take it.

—GEORGE MACDONALD

DEDICATED TO THE LORD

Lord, I humbly pray that I will be content with the
blessings You give. Help me to focus my thoughts
on living a dedicated life. Remind me that the
things I own do not define me. Almighty God, I am
delighted to have You as my Provider. Amen.

THE PERFECT FATHER

The first of all truths, which a lifetime of church going and Bible reading will fail to disclose, is that for life to be a good thing and worth living, a man must be the child of a perfect Father and know Him.

—GEORGE MACDONALD

EARLY DISPOSITIONS

A desire to be observed, considered, esteemed, praised, beloved, and admired by his fellows is one of the earliest as well as the keenest dispositions discovered in the heart of man.

—JOHN ADAMS

A BEAUTIFUL HOME

What is it that makes home so attractive? Is it because we have a beautiful home? Is it because we have beautiful lawns? . . . Is that all that makes home so attractive and so beautiful? Nay, it is the loved ones in it; it is the loved ones there.

—DWIGHT L. MOODY

A LOVE MESSAGE

If you want a love message to be heard, it has got
to be sent out. To keep a lamp burning, we have to
keep putting oil in it.

—MOTHER TERESA

CHANGE

Father, I often see that change is necessary for me to improve. If I do exactly the same thing each day in exactly the same way, then I should not expect results any different from the day before. Help me push beyond the mundane into the realm of active service. Amen.

BE GENUINE

You can fool all the people some of the time, and some of the people all the time, but you cannot fool all the people all the time.

—ABRAHAM LINCOLN

BUT ONCE. . .

I expect to pass through life but once. If therefore,
there be any kindness I can show, or any good thing
I can do to any fellow being, let me do it now,
and not defer or neglect it, as I shall not pass this
way again.

—WILLIAM PENN

RAISING BOYS

My father used to play with my brother and me in the yard. Mother would come out and say, "You're tearing up the grass."

"We're not raising grass," Dad would reply. "We're raising boys."

—HARMON KILLEBREW

SEEK TO BE USEFUL

If I know my own heart today, I would rather die than live as I once did, a mere nominal Christian, and not used by God in building up His kingdom. It seems a poor empty life to live for the sake of self. Let us seek to be useful. Let us seek to be vessels meet for the Master's use, that God, the Holy Spirit, may shine fully through us.

—DWIGHT L. MOODY

QUALITY TIME

Lord, I will monitor the routines of my children so that they do not become overloaded with activities that intrude on their time to grow spiritually. Help us to make quiet time for reflection and quality time for communicating with You. Amen.

What Is a Boy Worth?

Nobody knows what a boy is worth,
And the world must wait and see;
For every man in an honored place,
Is a boy that used to be.

—PHILLIPS BROOKS

BE HOME FOR DINNER

Even those for whom cooking is an oppressive
chore or a source of self-doubting anxiety
acknowledge that a meal shared by friends and
family is one of the bonding rituals without which
the family, society even, can fall apart.

—ANTONIA HILL

HARDSHIPS

I've had a hard life, but my hardships are nothing against the hardships that my father went through in order to get me to where I started.

—BERTRAND HUBBARD

MAKE LOVE CENTRAL

It is quite easy for me to think of a God of love
mainly because I grew up in a family where
love was central and where lovely relationships
were ever present.

—MARTIN LUTHER KING JR.

REST

"Come to me, all you who are weary and burdened, and I will give you rest. Take my yoke upon you and learn from me, for I am gentle and humble in heart, and you will find rest for your souls."

—MATTHEW 11:28–29 NIV

GOD IS LOVE

Riches take wings, comforts vanish, hope withers away, but love stays with us. God is love.

—LEW WALLACE

THE SMALL THINGS

Success in life is founded upon attention to the small things rather than to the large things; to the everyday things nearest to us rather than to the things that are remote and uncommon.

—BOOKER T. WASHINGTON

LET TROUBLE COME

My friends, if you go to the Lord with your troubles, He will take them away. Would you not rather be with the Lord and get rid of your troubles than be with your troubles and without God? Let trouble come if it will drive us nearer to God.

—DWIGHT L. MOODY

THE LAUGHTER
OF CHILDREN

Bricks and mortar make a house, but the laughter of children makes a home.

—IRISH PROVERB

ABUNDANT BLESSINGS

Lord, help me constantly monitor the spiritual condition of my children and myself.
Before our strength grows weak, please send heavenly refreshment to our souls and rejuvenate our worship. I pray that Your abundant blessings will continue to fall on my family and me. Amen.

FAMILY QUARRELS

Family quarrels are bitter things. They don't go
according to any rules. They're not like aches or
wounds: they're more like splits in the skin that
won't heal because there's not enough material.

—F. SCOTT FITZGERALD

PLACE EVERYTHING IN GOD'S HANDS

I have held many things in my hands, and I have lost them all; but whatever I have placed in God's hands, that I still possess.

—MARTIN LUTHER

THRIVING

If human beings are perceived as potentials rather than problems, as possessing strengths instead of weaknesses, as unlimited rather than dull and unresponsive, then they thrive and grow to their capabilities.

—BARBARA BUSH

A STRENGTH THAT NEVER FAILS

Faith is an outward look. Faith does not look within; it looks without. It is not what I think nor what I feel nor what I have done, but it is what Jesus Christ is and has done, and so we should trust in Him who is our strength, and whose strength will never fail.

—DWIGHT L. MOODY

STRIVE ON

With malice toward none, with charity for all,
with firmness in the right, as God gives us to see
the right, let us strive on to finish the work we
are in.

—ABRAHAM LINCOLN

FAMILY

We need to love our family for who they are and not for what they do.

—KAREN McDUFFY

ADVENTURE

Bringing up a family should be an adventure, not an anxious discipline in which everybody is constantly graded for performance.

—MILTON R. SAPERSTEIN

WITH ALL MY HEART

I am tired and sick of halfheartedness. I don't like a halfhearted man. I don't care for anyone to love me halfheartedly. And the Lord won't have it. If we are going to seek for Him and find Him, we must do it with all our hearts.

—DWIGHT L. MOODY

SPACE

Family: A social unit where the father is concerned with parking space, the children with outer space, and the mother with closet space.

—EVAN ESAR

Be Faithful Today

Heavenly Father, please help me to keep my focus on You today. I don't need to worry about tomorrow or fret over the past. All I need to concern myself with right now is being faithful today. Amen.

A Reminder

God has given you your child, that the sight of him, from time to time, might remind you of His goodness and induce you to praise Him with filial reverence.

—CHRISTIAN SCRIVER

ATTITUDE

The only thing we can do is play on the one
string we have, and that is our attitude. . . . I am
convinced that life is 10 percent what happens to
me and 90 percent how I react to it.

—CHARLES SWINDOLL

KEEP YOUR EYES
ON THE MASTER

The moment he got his eye off the Master, he failed; and every man, I don't care who he is— even the strongest—every man that hasn't Christ in him is a failure.

—DWIGHT L. MOODY

WORTH IT

When I say. . ."I am a Christian," I'm not claiming to be perfect. My flaws are far too visible, but God believes I am worth it.

—MAYA ANGELOU

A BLESSING FOR YOUR CHILDREN

The just man walketh in his integrity: his children are blessed after him.

—PROVERBS 20:7 KJV

BE ALL THERE

Wherever you are, *be all there*. Live to the hilt
every situation you believe to be the will of God.

—JIM ELLIOT

LIVE FULLY

Lord, I pray in Your name that You would allow me to live fully in every situation You put me in. Help me to be "all there" when my children need me to listen. Amen.

GOD AND ANGELS

Reputation is what men and women think of us; character is what God and angels know of us.

—THOMAS PAINE

THE PEACE OF GOD

Sometimes I am amazed to see how little it takes
to drive all peace and comfort from some people.
Some slandering tongue will readily blast it. But if
we have the peace of God, the world cannot take
that from us.

—DWIGHT L. MOODY

THANK YOU, LORD

Father, I want to thank You for Your many
blessings. As I head into the next chapter of my
life, help me to lead my family with courage and a
strong faith in You. Amen.

NOTES